Losing My Guardian Angel: A Short Poetic Journey

Benji Leigh

BookLeaf Publishing

India | USA | UK

Presentation by *BookLeaf Publishing*

Web: www.bookleafpub.com

E-mail: info@bookleafpub.com

ISBN: 9789358735161

First edition 2023

ACKNOWLEDGEMENT

All of the staff at Somerset and Blue Pearl who helped care for my sweetheart while she was sick. She was well attended to and kept comfortable.

Somerset for their beautiful, heartfelt card with a message from everyone, as well as the set of pawprints they took for me. Their compassion means the world.

The countless friends and family who supported me during this time.

The band Nothing More, whose music has helped me through hard times for many years. Their music heals.

And to everyone who ever loved her, which is really everyone who ever met her.

Vacancy

I wake up
and reach for her.
It is too quiet

in this place
my dog used to call home.

In her absence,
I am filled
with emptiness.

perhaps I'll find her
looking for me, too.

Shut Up, You Gorgeous German Shepherd

A rogue squirrel,
buffed up trees,
the obnoxious barking next door -

one less little life,

not here to enjoy
the bliss
of a peaceful afternoon on the deck.

Suffocation

How, exactly,
does this work?
My soul is trapped

in a volcano -
And I am waiting,
here, for it to erupt.

How did I get here?

Angry smoke billows past me
And I struggle to take a
breath.

Where Is She?

Words dance across the screen
inside my mind.
BOLDED, ALL CAPS,
flashing behind
my eyes.

My aching soul asks -
where did she go?
The question bounces around my head
until it is all I can see.
Where is my guardian angel?

Intrusive Thoughts

It creeps around
the crypts of my mind

and my eyes
won't let me cry.

My heart feels trapped
in a cast of fiberglass.

With a heavy sigh -
My head

bangs against the wall.
And it goes

until I am able
to breathe again.

Out Of My Way, Motherfucker

The zoomies are a beautiful thing.
I miss the way she would grin,
The way her butt wiggled,
The way she looked at me.

In her absence
my heart feels ripped open,
and yet - I remember
How she would zoom,

zoom, zoom.
Making the cutest little sounds -
arr, ruff! arr, ruff!
The zoomies are a beautiful thing.

The Sun Is Down

Bright orange sunrise -
such a calming atmosphere
to remember her.

What I wouldn't give
To see trash across my floor
One more fucking time.

In Her Absence

8

I'm aware,
always,
of something
flat.
devoid.
Something that
makes my soul
ache.

In the night
it gets louder.
And louder.
Who knew
absence
could scream?

Dancing Feet

Paws
across the hardwood -
A sound

more majestic
than opera
or tap dancing.

The high-pitched
yips and yaps
that make me

sigh heavily with annoyance,
and smile, softly, out of love.
All she wants

is to go for a walk
with her human,
and she simply

cannot
stop
wiggling.

Her innocence
and her passion
warm my soul.

A Storm Is Coming

Gray streaks across the sky -
With heavy gusts,
the trees

rattle and sway
As the atmosphere
gears up for battle.

I stand outside
under the deck,
feeling the stormy wind

ripple across my skin.
A branch falls.
The sky has darkened;

I look up
and take a
deep breath.

It's Not That Easy

Death is the end
of a relationship.

But it's not as if I can just
block her number,

or delete our texts,
or unfriend her.

This relationship
is entirely primal

Her essence, it
lives within me.

and no matter what
I cannot forget her.

Spiritual Questions

I just woke up
without her in my bed.
No morning yawns
with the dog breath.
No cuddles,
no kisses,
no love.

As much as I will
always cherish
my days with her -
right now, this feels as if
my heart has been
plopped into a vat of sulfuric acid.

corrosive chemicals spitting
over me and my memories.
I am blessed -
to have been loved
by such an angel.

I'm not sure who I am
in her absence
And I desperately wish I knew
what's happened to her soul.

Does she visit me
and I just can't tell?
would my soul

feel her presence?
Is she, as some say,

truly here with me, always?

Those Damn Nocturnal Bugs

Some kind of
objectionable bug
chatters in the night.
I sit by the window,
eyes
begrudgingly open.

In old times,
a tiny little
heating pad
would lull me back to sleep.
My sweet, warm girl
can't help me now.

Distraction

15

Lusting over something
you will never get -
thinking about it

nonstop,
missing out
on the present.

Wishing, wishing,
it would go away.
Hoping
something comes of it.
This is how I
grieve.

My logic-brain knows
I can't have her back.
But, much like lust,

grief itches.

Strike, You're Out

There is so much
to be said
about loss.

It is a bowling ball
obliterating
all ten pins at once.

I know that grief
is a reflection
of love.

but that
isn't keeping me
from falling apart.

Volcanic Ash

Just barely, enough
of the despair
has dissipated,

and I can finally consider - what
do I do

with her ashes?
She should be
honored

by my decision.
So much
could be done.

I hope
there is no
wrong choice.

Sunny Day

I can feel your hot breath
across my face
as I remember;
those times that

going outside made you so happy.
I think often about
the grin across your face,
how you'd bark and bark,

to be let outside
and enjoy the sun.
Then you'd dart inside
and do all you could

to climb
up me
in search
of love.

A Mangrove Forest

Like a mangrove shows its roots,
she showed me her soul.
I cherish that more
than words can do justice.
The pure trust,
the unconditional love,
the priceless connection.
Dogs - they have
such beautiful souls.

Angel Versus Mammoth

As I attempt to learn
how to stay afloat
without my little love,
I realize:

she had a mammoth
of a job.
My angel slayed
my demons
like it was nothing.

The labyrinth
of my mind
proves itself
confounding

to me.
Freeze mode
grabs me
by the throat

and makes me forget
to breathe.
I'm so grateful
to have had her.

The Ethereal Mirror

21

The image of her
in the mirror
next to me

is fading.
She knew
how to take me

and my bullshit -
and create peace.
I don't want

my memories
of her
to dissolve.

Her peace
kept me sane
for so long.

My & My Shadow

The pieces of my heart
are still shuffled around
in my chest;
A few have found
their way home,
but many are still
lost
without her.

As the puzzle
that is my heart
slowly puts itself
back together,
I search for a sense
of equanimity.

It's just me
and my shadow, now,
but I know my little
guardian angel

believes that I
will be okay.